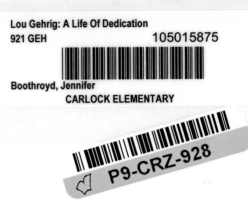

Lou Gehrig
A LIFE OF DEDICATION

by Jennifer Boothroyd

Lerner Publications Company • Minneapolis

Photo Acknowledgments

The images in this book are used with the permission of: Comstock Images, p. 4; © Hulton Archive/Getty Images, p. 6; © Underwood & Underwood/CORBIS, p. 8; Library of Congress, p. 9 (LC-DIG-ggbain-03234); National Baseball Hall of Fame Library, Cooperstown, N.Y., pp. 10, 12, 16, 20, 26; © Bettmann/CORBIS, pp. 11, 14, 18; © Mark Rucker/Transcendental Graphics, Getty Images, pp. 15, 25; AP Photo, pp. 19, 22, 24; AP story on page 15 of The Baltimore Sun, Wednesday Morning Edition, May 3, 1939, p. 23.

Front Cover: © Mark Rucker/Transcendental Graphics, Getty Images.

Text copyright © 2008 by Lerner Publishing Group, Inc.

Lerner Publications Company
A division of Lerner Publishing Group, Inc.
241 First Avenue North
Minneapolis, MN 55401 U.S.A.

Website address: www.lernerbooks.com

Words in **bold type** are explained in a glossary on page 31.

Library of Congress Cataloging-in-Publication Data

Boothroyd, Jennifer, 1972–
    Lou Gehrig : a life of dedication / by Jennifer Boothroyd.
      p.   cm. – (Pull ahead books biographies)
    Includes index.
    ISBN: 978-0-8225-8587-9 (lib. bdg. : alk. paper)
    1. Gehrig, Lou, 1903–1941–Juvenile literature. 2. Baseball players–United States–Biography–Juvenile literature. 3. New York Yankees (Baseball team)–Juvenile literature.
    I. Title.
    GV865.G4B66 2008
    796.357092–dc22[B]   2007024880

Manufactured in the United States of America
1 2 3 4 5 6 – JR – 13 12 11 10 09 08

Table of Contents

4

Hard Work

Imagine getting a perfect score on your weekly spelling test. Does that sound impossible? **Dedication** can make it happen. Dedicated people work hard to reach their goals. Lou Gehrig was very dedicated. His dedication made him one of baseball's greatest players.

New York City, about 1903

Growing Up

Lou Gehrig was born on June 19, 1903, in New York City. His family was poor. Lou's mother washed laundry for other people. Lou dedicated himself to helping his mother. He picked up the dirty clothes from their owners and returned them when they were clean.

Lou was also dedicated to his favorite sport, baseball.

Lou's favorite baseball player was Honus Wagner *(left)*.

Kids play on a street in New York City in 1909.

Lou and his friends got up early many mornings to play a game of baseball. Then they would go to school.

Lou is fourteen years old in this school photo.

School was hard for Lou. But he was dedicated to his schoolwork. He always tried his best.

Lou was on his high school's baseball team. He hit the ball very well. Lou hit many **home runs**.

Lou (*circled*) and his high school baseball team

Lou played baseball for Columbia University.

Paid to Play

After high school, Lou played baseball in college. The New York Yankees baseball team heard how well Lou played. They offered Lou a job playing baseball. Lou was very happy. He wanted to pay his parents' bills with the money he **earned**.

Lou did not get to play in many games.
Professional baseball was harder
than the games he played in school.

Lou *(circled)* and the 1923 New York Yankees

Lou practices with his teammate Babe Ruth.

Lou practiced whenever he could.
He was **determined** to keep his job
playing for the Yankees.

A Place to Stay

Lou's hard work helped him reach his goal. In 1925, he started at first base. Lou played hard for his team. It did not matter if he was tired or hurt. He knew his team was counting on him to play.

Lou's dedication made him a popular player for the Yankees. His home runs helped the team win many games and six **World Series**.

Lou hits a home run during the 1928 World Series.

Lou's mother, wife, and father watch a Yankees game.

Lou also took care of his family. He made sure they had everything they needed.

20

Doesn't Feel Right

In 1939, Lou felt that something was wrong with his body. He had trouble hitting a ball. He could not run quickly to the bases. Lou knew he wasn't helping the team. He told the coach to let someone else play.

Lou *(right)* talks to the teammate who will play for him.

At the next game, everyone was surprised. This would be the first game without Lou in fourteen **seasons**.

Lou had played 2,130 games in a row.
No player had ever done that before.

GEHRIG HALTS RECORD STREAK

Benches Himself After Playing In 2,130 Consecutive Games

[By the Associated Press]

Detroit, May 2--For the first time since May 30, 1925, the New York Yankees played a major league baseball game today without Lou Gehrig in the lineup.

Apparently without regret, Gehrig ended his amazing "iron man" performance at 2,130 consecutive games for what he termed "the good o' the team"

Lou went to the doctor to find out what was wrong. The doctor told Lou he had a disease called ALS.

Lou talks to a doctor about ALS.

Lou *(center)* says good-bye to his fans and teammates.

ALS makes a person's muscles very
weak. Lou could not play baseball
anymore.

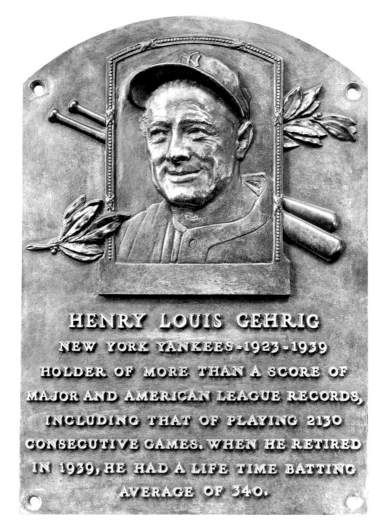

HENRY LOUIS GEHRIG
NEW YORK YANKEES·1923·1939
HOLDER OF MORE THAN A SCORE OF
MAJOR AND AMERICAN LEAGUE RECORDS,
INCLUDING THAT OF PLAYING 2130
CONSECUTIVE GAMES. WHEN HE RETIRED
IN 1939, HE HAD A LIFE TIME BATTING
AVERAGE OF 340.

Lou's plaque in the National Baseball Hall of Fame

A Lasting Legend

Lou Gehrig died on June 2, 1941, from ALS. Lou was dedicated to both his family and baseball. He tried his best because he knew people were counting on him. His dedication made him a great baseball player and earned him the respect of others.

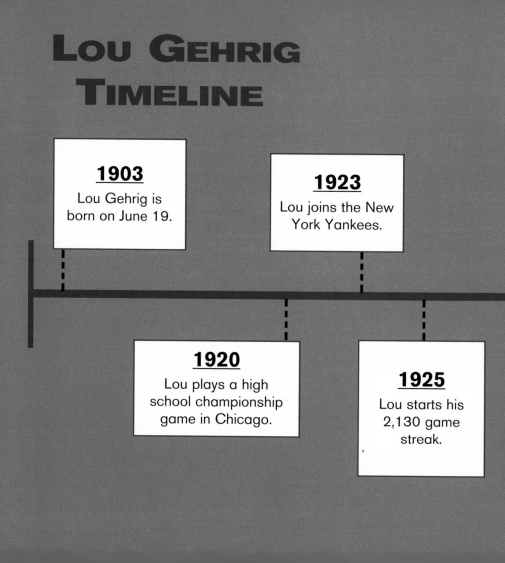

LOU GEHRIG TIMELINE

1903
Lou Gehrig is born on June 19.

1923
Lou joins the New York Yankees.

1920
Lou plays a high school championship game in Chicago.

1925
Lou starts his 2,130 game streak.

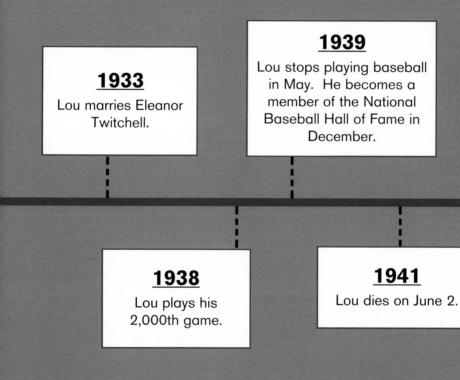

1933
Lou marries Eleanor Twitchell.

1939
Lou stops playing baseball in May. He becomes a member of the National Baseball Hall of Fame in December.

1938
Lou plays his 2,000th game.

1941
Lou dies on June 2.

More about Lou Gehrig

● Lou married Eleanor Twitchell on the morning of September 29, 1933. After the ceremony, he rushed to the stadium to play an afternoon game.

● When Lou left baseball, his team decided that no other Yankees player could have Lou's uniform number. That was the first time a baseball player's number was retired.

● In 1995, Cal Ripken Jr. broke Lou's record of playing 2,130 games in a row.

Websites

Lou Gehrig
http://www.answers.com/topic/lou-gehrig

Lou Gehrig: National Baseball Hall of Fame
http://www.baseballhalloffame.org/hofers/detail.jsp
?playerId=114680

Lou Gehrig: The Official Website
http://www.lougehrig.com/

Glossary

dedication: giving a lot of time and effort to something or someone

determined: firm in sticking to a purpose

earned: got by working

home runs: hits that let baseball players touch all the bases in one turn and score a run

professional: getting paid to do something instead of doing it as a hobby

seasons: the months when baseball games are played each year

World Series: the games played between two teams for the baseball championship

Index